The Law

~

How to Apply the Law of Attraction to Channel Your Energy to Reach All Your Goals in Life

~

Use LOA to Improve Your Relationships, Career, Health & Fitness, Love and Happiness

Sam Willis

First Published 2015

~

Copyright © 2015 Sam Willis

All rights reserved.

ISBN-10: 1512351032
ISBN-13: **978-1512351033**

CONTENTS

	Introduction	4
1	What is the Law of Attraction	6
2	The Basic Principles of the Law of Attraction	9
3	Follow These Three Simple Yet Powerful Tips	13
4	Why People Fail	17
5	Attract the Love You Want	20
6	Attract More Money	27
7	Powerful Affirmations to Attract Happiness	30
	Conclusion	38

Introduction

I want to thank you and congratulate you for purchasing this book:

The Law of Attraction: How to Apply the Law of Attraction to Channel Your Energy to Reach All Your Goals in Life.

This book will help you understand the principles of the Law of Attraction. You will also learn how to activate this universal law in your life in three easy steps.

The book also gives insights on why some people fail despite following the basic principles of the Law of Attraction; at the same time you will learn ways to achieve your goals using this law.

If you are looking for love, this book also teaches you how to attract your soul mate. And you will learn to attract more money with easy-to-follow strategies.

Lastly, you will be given powerful affirmations to achieve true happiness and improve your life.

CHAPTER 1

What is the Law of Attraction?

The Law of Attraction is one of the most popular universal laws. The main theory behind this law is that *people create their own realities*. You attract what you want but you also unconsciously attract what you don't want. You attract the people that you have in your life right now, whether they have done you good or not. Likewise, you attract the stuff that you have in your own home. You attract either wealth or poverty.

Simply put, everything that is happening in your life, whatever you have, and whoever you have in your life right now, are results of your own doing and have manifested through your own thoughts and feelings.

Therefore, if you have limited beliefs, you attract limited wealth, thereby compromising your wellbeing. On the other hand, if you believe that everything and anything is possible, you attract success. When you don't set limitations on what you can achieve, you can achieve far greater things.

You see, focusing on the things that you don't have doesn't make things better for you; if you look at the Law of Attraction, focusing on the things you lack only attracts negativity and limitations, so you still end up with nothing. You create your own reality, so if you focus on wealth and abundance, you attract those things.

Much has been written about this powerful law and if you take all of their principles, you still arrive at the same basic principle—you make the life you want.

Understanding the Law of Attraction

You probably have heard a friend talk about the Law of Attraction, or you know someone who seems to have perfected the art of manifesting. There is probably someone you know whom you feel a little envious of because he or she seemingly has a monopoly when it comes to wealth and abundance.

It is possible that most of the people who seem to have everything in life may have perfected the art of manifesting. When you think about the Law of Attraction, you need to go back to its main theory: *you attract what you want.*

So, if you want to attract wealth, you have to think of abundance, wealth, and the good life.

Attracting Abundance Is Knowledge Itself

The "knowledge" of manifesting is no different than playing the guitar or knowing how to read notes. Manifesting is like any other skill that you learn and perfect. How good you are at something will depend on how efficient you have become at doing or performing it. While some people may be better than you in certain skills, it doesn't mean that you cannot improve; with a lot of practice, you surely can.

Going back to the power of manifesting, those people who have become efficient at attracting whatever they want have trained their minds to focus on their own desires. It has become so natural to them that they don't even realize how they do it.

How do they do it? How can you manifest the life you want? How can you attract the good things in life?

The Law of Attraction

Understanding the Law of Attraction is the first step to living the life you want.

You are responsible for whatever you attract in your own life. Whatever you have in your life right now, whether you are living comfortably or not, it is all your doing. You attract those things: relationships, friends, money, and employment.

When the Law of Attraction is being discussed, the power of affirmations also comes into place.

What are Affirmations?

Affirmations are sentences that you speak (or read) over and over to influence your way of thinking. These are powerful words that can motivate you to keep your mind focused on a specific goal. When used correctly, they can greatly influence your subconscious mind.

Affirmations have the power to change the way you think and the way you behave. They can bring you to the right people who can help you achieve your goals and dreams.

They have to be positive statements so that you feel and think positive, thus putting you in a better position to transform both your inner and outside worlds.

Affirmations can be about anything: success, happiness, health, money, or relationships.

CHAPTER 2

The Basic Principles of the Law of Attraction

In order to better understand the Law of Attraction, you will need to know the principles of the said law. If you have a better understanding, it will be easier to use it to your advantage.

Understand Vibrations

You know what sympathetic vibrations are? Take two "Middle C" tuning forks for instance. If you lay them side-by-side, hit just one of them, you can be sure that the other one will vibrate as the one you touched vibrates. Simply put, sympathetic vibrations are similar poles—they attract.

Similarly, the Law of Attraction states that everything in the Universe vibrates. So, as something vibrates, it attracts anything that has the same wavelength. Take humans for example, people vibrate feelings. Whatever you think about, you bring about. So, if you are having negative thoughts, you will be sending out negative feelings as well; as a result, you will attract the same negativity that you are sending out to the Universe.

Consequently, when you think about positive things, you feel good and you attract the same positivity. Those feelings attract things within the same wavelength.

If you want to use the power of the Law of Attraction in your favor, change your thoughts and fill your mind with only positive things.

You Have to Increase Your Vibrations

It is important to reiterate that there are only two types of feelings in this world—the good and the bad. Remember when you woke up one morning in a really bad mood? Did you notice that your day spiraled downward just because you woke up on the other side of the bed?

Picture this: you slept through your alarm, you tore off a button on your shirt, you missed the bus, you came in late for work, and you got reprimanded by your boss. All these happened because you didn't have a good mood when you woke up that morning.

The Law of Attraction will only respond to whatever emotions you put out. In this case, you've had negative emotions (or low vibrations) when you woke up so you attracted the negative energy.

Now think about the times when you woke up feeling good and happy. Do you remember how your day turned out? You had a great breakfast, you arrived at the office earlier than usual, you closed a big account, and you got promoted because of that.

Can you see the difference now? Never underestimate the power of the subconscious. Make it a point to wake up each morning with a happy disposition, and see how your day changes. It doesn't matter if you woke up on the wrong side of the bed; you can change your mood.

You Have the Power to Change Your Mood

If you ever wake up not feeling so good, remember that you have the option to stay that way or change it. You have the power to make that switch. You can either smile through the bad mood by thinking about the things that make you happy, like your favorite dessert, seeing your pet, or getting a peck from your kids. The power is within you to control whatever mood you will have the whole day.

You might have often heard this phrase being said over and over: happiness is a choice! It is indeed a choice. You can either choose to be happy or miserable each morning when you open your eyes. It's your choice, so choose wisely!

Follow the Four-Step Process of Deliberate Creation

1. Identify the things that you *don't* want to have or to happen.

2. Get a clear picture of what you actually want.

3. Feel what it is like if you have already gotten what you want.

4. Allow the Universe to deliver to you the things that you want.

How it Works

If you will be following the Law of Attraction, there shouldn't be any doubt clouding the things that you are supposed to be doing. Allow its principles to work for you. Believe that the Universe can actually bring you whatever it is you desire. Allow the law to manifest your wants, your desires, and your goals. If you are clouded even with the slightest of doubts, the Universe will get mixed signals and it won't be able to give you what you want.

When you allow the Law of Attraction to work, you have to give it your full trust; believe that the Universe is capable of giving you the desires of your heart.

The Three-Step Strategy to Get What You Want

There is a creative process that will work well with the Law of Attraction:

1. *Ask* – The first step is to ask for what you want. In order to make this work, you have to know what you really want. The Universe won't be able to bring you what you want if

you yourself are not sure what you exactly want. Does it make sense?

2. *Believe* - If you ask for it, believe that you deserve to have it and that it will be given to you. There shouldn't be any room for doubt.

3. *Receive* – It is one thing to ask and to believe, but you also have to be an active player in reaching for your goals. When opportunity knocks, grab it at first instance.

CHAPTER 3

Follow These Three Simple Yet Powerful Tips

Are you still wondering how you can make your own reality by applying the Law of Attraction in your own life?

Manifesting is your ability to attract positive things by using your own thoughts and intentions. Its principles have been in existence for centuries and have been used by people across all cultures and civilizations.

The main principle of manifesting lies in the fact that everything in this world is composed of particles of energy which are vibrating at varying frequencies.

Sending out positive thoughts will bring about positive energy. Likewise, if you send out negative thoughts, you will only attract negative energy, and you don't want that to happen.

Everyone uses manifestation in their own lives, be it consciously or unconsciously. But, most of the time, you unconsciously do it. Remember the time when you experienced one success after another? How about when things weren't going your way and everything was spiraling downwards?

You may not be aware of it, but you are already manifesting the

Law of Attraction in your own life. You will learn more about how you can use this universal law to work to your advantage.

It takes a lot of practice to become aware of your thoughts and feelings, but when you are able to master it, you will be able to tap into the real power of your mind.

Master the art of manifesting and this powerful law with these three basic but very powerful tricks:

1. Clarity

What is your usual response when people ask you what you want to have in your life? Are you like most people whose general answers are, *I want to find happiness* or *I want to find success?*

If you answer that way, see how you are in your life right now. Are you happy? Are you successful? It is necessary to be clear about the meaning of happiness and success *for you*; otherwise, you won't be able to find what you're looking for.

If you want to manifest your hopes and dreams, you have to have a clear vision of what you really want. When you know exactly what your desires are, it is easier to fill your mind with vivid thoughts and pictures of all the things that you want to happen in your life.

If you want to attract happiness, you have to have a clear understanding of what makes you happy. For instance, it's possible that happiness for you is to meet the man of your dreams. You have to be clear about what the man of your dreams is going to be like, not just the looks but the "overall package." If you want to attract all the right people, you have to make your thoughts about them as clear as possible.

When your mind is clear, you also have a clear understanding of what you are passionate about. A clear mind is passionate about the things that you want to achieve; because of this clarity, you are able to focus on the things that you are passionate about.

So, if you want to manifest something in your life, take a moment to define and clarify your goals. You may begin with one goal at a time. Use your five senses to throw out into the Universe what you want to happen in your life. Let your senses determine what you'll feel, hear, see, and experience, when your goal(s) become reality.

When your emotions, thoughts, and your whole being can create a strong magnetizing effect that is sent out to the Universe, you are also creating a powerful magnetizing effect in the fulfillment of your goals.

2. Write Them Down

Put all your dreams, goals, and aspirations into writing, similar to your daily affirmations. Why should you put them in writing? It helps you to focus on your goals. Every time you read your list, you are reminded of them.

Recent studies have revealed that an average of 33% of people who put their goals into writing end up manifesting them into reality. It is one thing to formulate your goals, but stating them is another thing. Remember, it is not enough to have an idea of what you want; you have to be clear about the things so that when you write them down, you know exactly what you want because you can see them in your mind.

3. The Power of Gratitude

If you are always thankful for what you have, more will be given to you. Imbibe an *attitude of gratitude* and you'll achieve a positive mindset that will align your energy with the natural flow of joy, happiness, and prosperity. The more positive your thoughts are, and the more your emotions are aligned with those thoughts, the faster you will achieve abundance.

Be thankful even for the little things. You can begin by writing down the names of at least five people, situations, or things that you are most thankful for. You can also jot down whatever happened to you during the day that you are thankful for. Practice doing this each night before going to sleep.

Practicing gratitude can effectively shift your negative energy to positive energy. When you are thankful for anything and everything (even the challenges), you clear out the negative energy so you can still end up being positive. It is always a matter of perspective. Difficulties and adversities need not result in negative vibrations if you only look at them differently.

So, how do you begin activating the Law of Attraction in your life? *Be clear* with your goals, *put them into writing*, and develop an *attitude of gratitude* all the time.

CHAPTER 4

Why Some People Fail

Why do some people fail to manifest their hopes and dreams despite using the principles of the Law of Attraction? This chapter explains the things that other people might be doing wrong.

Creating an intention is necessary in manifesting your goals. Intention has two primary components: *content* and *energy*.

The *content* of the intention is the information about your desires. Content is whatever you want to manifest, such as earning an extra $5,000 a month, finding a better relationship, or getting a new career.

Energy is how you bring about your intentions. People think that it is a feeling, like passion. However, the feeling is really the result of the energy. You know that there is energy when you are able to connect very strong feelings with your goals.

You'll learn more about energy in the latter part of this chapter, but first, let us look into the content of your intention.

It Is Not Enough to Just Have Good Content

Some people continue to wonder why they have failed despite correctly applying the principles of the Law of Attraction. They wonder why their intentions did not manifest. What could have gone wrong?

The number one reason why people fail is that they assume that content alone will bring about the realization of their desires. Content is not enough because energy is the second important component of manifesting.

Good content without energy will not "fly" and will only lead to frustration and disappointment.

It is like writing excellent content for your blog but when you are about to publish it, the electricity goes down. How will you be able to make your message known?

Without Energy, Content Is Nothing

The energy of the intention is not the same as electricity, but it is an excellent metaphor to help you understand the concept.

Most people assume that the energy of the intention is the emotional juice that you bring to the intention. Truth is, it is a part of it, but you have to keep in mind that strong emotions are actually the result of that energy.

If you want to understand it more clearly, look at the children. They are actually "intention-manifestation" masters! When kids want something badly, they will go to their parents and ask for it. They'll do anything for their parents to take notice and eventually give in to their wants. They will jump around and drive everyone crazy until they are given what they want. They will not give up until they have gotten what they want.

Examine yourself; are you like those kids when pursuing your goals and dreams? What type of energy do you bring into your intentions? Do you think and speak about them like they mean the world to you? Are you pumped up with so much emotion that you cannot contain your enthusiasm about the thought of getting what you want?

You don't have to take it literally and throw a tantrum each time. What you have to do is to feel passionately about your intention. Be excited! Be enthusiastic!

Strong emotions are not the cause, but rather the result of energy. Emotions actually let you know how much energy you are able to put into your intention.

What's the real source of the energy of intention? The source is actually the Universe! The energy has always been there; you just need to tap into it with your intention. Like electricity, it is always there, you just need to activate it—like turning on the light or powering on your appliances.

Energy works like that. Since it is out there, you only need to "plug" into it with your intentions. Energy is nothing until you tap into it. That is something that most people fail to realize. You have to keep the energy flowing.

CHAPTER 5

Attract the Love You Want

If you are a hopeless romantic, you believe there is someone meant for you – a soul mate. It's likely though, that you'll end up meeting several "wrong ones" before meeting "the one." What if you have had enough heartbreak and you feel hopeless already? Don't fret, because this chapter gives you effective steps for attracting your soul mate.

How to Manifest Your Soul Mate

1. Be Committed

   The idea of being committed is to become one with your mind. Commitment is your willingness to give your time and energy to an idea or to something that you believe in, that it becomes a part of your whole being. You work towards achieving a goal every moment of your life – that is commitment.

   People generally have an idea of what they are looking for in a future partner. You probably have a clear idea of what your soul mate would be like: beautiful, charming, intelligent, caring, thoughtful, and the list goes on. Think about it; what if there is someone, who has all those qualities looking at you and looking for the same qualities. Would that person see those qualities in you? Would that person be interested in getting to know you? If not, then you have your work cut out for you.

You see, for you to attract the love you want, you have to be someone that you want to be with. If you have not found someone with the above qualities, chances are you are not the same person either. You have to work on being the "right one" before you can find "the one."

Commitment is becoming the person you want to attract first, and then everything follows.

Manifesting Your Soul Mate Should Be Your Own Journey

Committing to finding your soul mate means you are ready to go to the next level of your evolution. You are ready to discover the gifts that will be given to you, at the same time, doing the same for another person. In essence, you will be supporting each other's journey.

This is not a journey of finally meeting your soul mate but rather a journey of discovering your own qualities and eventually learning to love yourself, before welcoming another person's love. Manifesting is becoming your own person first, accepting everything about you, both the good and the bad.

Are you ready to commit right now? If you are, then say this to yourself with your hand placed on your heart, *"I, (your name), am fully committing to welcoming my soul mate. I also fully commit to grow into someone I want to fall in love with."*

2. You Should Have a Clear Image of What Your Soul Mate Is Going to Be Like

Have you thought about what your soul mate would look like? Have you thought about what qualities he/she would possess? What are the things that will attract you to him/her? Most people begin the journey of finding a soul mate by establishing what they *don't* want. This is why they often fail to find "the one" because they dwell on the negative aspect of it all.

The point in having clarity is in knowing what you want. If you have a clear vision of what you want in a soul mate, it will be easier to identify that person the moment you see and hear him/her. Most important of all, you should have a clear vision so that you won't get lost in a relationship with someone other than your soul mate.

Focus on the things that you want; think of someone who will have the same values that you have. The first step to gaining clarity is to create three lists:

- *The first is the "soul mate list."* You will list the attributes and qualities that you want your soul mate to have. This is the "what-you-want-your-soul mate-to-be" list. Jot down all the characteristics and physical attributes that you want your soul mate to possess. Include qualities like loving, caring, committed, healthy, etc.

- *Your next list is the "deal breaker list."* This list will consist of the things that would turn you off in a person. List three characteristics that would make you turn away and consider not having a relationship with him/her. Your list could include, alcohol addiction, substance abuse, or committed to someone else.

- *Your third list will be "your gifts" list.* Remember that your soul mate is not someone who will rescue you from your misery. Your soul mate should be someone with whom you will share the rest of your life. Your soul mate is someone you will love, support, and nurture—just as he/she will love, support, and nurture you. This third list is all about you; think of what you will bring to the relationship, not the other way around.

3. Make That "Soul Call"

This is a process that is used to find a connection to your soul mate, without having to meet each other.

Before everything is manifested in the Universe, it begins from an inner plane of emotions, thoughts, and ideas. There is proof that people who are far apart and haven't even met, can affect each other's thoughts, heartbeat, and ability to love just by simply having thoughts about each other.

You and your soul mate have to "meet" on that inner plane, before you can draw him/her toward you. It comes easy with these steps:

- *Set your intention.* You can either say it or put it into writing. Say or write something like this, *"I am ready to open my heart. I openly welcome love to reside in my heart."*

- *Have an open mind.* Firmly believe that your soul mate is out there waiting for you. Believe that nothing and no one can keep you apart. You can say, *"My soul mate is coming my way and I am ready."*

- *Have an open heart.* Visualize what your soul mate will look like. Be aware of how you will feel if you have finally met him/her. You might have met your soul mate but you just haven't realized that he/she is "the one."

4. Clear or Smooth Out the Dents

Keep in mind that spiritual growth begins when you let go of your old ways and embrace new aspects of yourself. Welcoming someone with an open heart and mind is part of growing spiritually. Once you start with the process, you will also have to begin clearing out the dents. This means that you have to begin removing whatever obstacles might be keeping you from getting the relationship you want.

Here are steps on how you can clear any built up obstacles:

- *Start with the healing of your heart.* Along life's road, you will experience happiness and heartaches. If you are still holding on to the pain of the past, it is now time to begin the healing process so that you can have room as you welcome your soul mate. Start the healing process by forgiving the people who have hurt you. It is also important that you forgive yourself for whatever mistakes you have made that have hurt you and the people around you. Begin the healing now!

- *Clear your mind.* When you begin with the healing process, you also have to free your mind of any belief and fear that may be keeping you from welcoming the love that you deserve. Let go of the negative thoughts. Never think that you aren't good enough, or that no one can love an overweight woman/man; if you're a single parent, don't ever assume that no one would fall for you. Let go of these beliefs and fears. A soul mate will love you unconditionally and you will also feel the same way towards him/her.

- *Let go of the past.* Are you still hoping to get back with your former lover? Do you still love your ex? If you want to finally attract "the one," you have to stop looking back at your past relationships. You have to free your heart so that the one who is meant for you will have space to enter. *Let go!*

- *Make room in your life for "the one."* Are you ready for a loving and healthy relationship? Can you make room for your soul mate? Maybe you have been single for quite a while and you have been working so hard that you don't really have the time to go out and meet people. Maybe you are settling for casual relationships. What if you meet your soul mate today? Are you ready? If you really want to meet "the one," you have to make sure that you have room for him/her in your life; otherwise, the opportunity might pass you by.

5. Begin Telling a New Story

Are you still hung up with the last person who broke your heart? Do you still dwell on the memories of a painful breakup? If you want to attract your soul mate, you have to begin telling a new story. Begin telling the story of how magical it is going to be when you finally meet your soul mate.

6. Get Help from the Right People

Life is a challenge for most people. Life is a series of ups and downs. There will be some good times and there will be some bad times. You will need a support system to help you in your journey to finally meeting your soul mate. You need support from friends and family. In order to fully heal from past hurts, you might need to get the help of a therapist, a counselor, or a coach.

Remember, soul mates come into your life to heal your deepest emotional wounds; well, you come into their lives to do the same. However, you need to grow first as an individual before you can grow with someone else. Your support group would be able to help you with that.

Keep in mind, though, to include in your support group, only those who are trustworthy and can bring about positive energy. The last thing you need is a skeptic who wouldn't believe in whatever you want to accomplish.

7. Be Ready!

If you believe you can manifest, you have to be ready when your soul mate arrives. Trust the process and keep in mind that nothing can keep you and your soul mate away from each other.

At this point, "divine and perfect timing" will be working to put you and your soul mate at the right place, at the right time for the two of you to meet. Use your time of waiting to grow so that when your soul mate finally comes, you are ready. Learn to fully love yourself. Enjoy singlehood. Follow your heart.

Be open to all the possibilities and follow all the maps that may lead you to your soul mate; remember the Universe will be working for that one perfect time!

CHAPTER 6

Attract More Money

Everyone wants to live comfortably and in abundance. If you want to attract more money into your life, the following tips will be helpful:

Know Exactly What You Want

Just like in attracting the love you want, you have to be clear on exactly what you want. Say it, name it, and claim that you already have it. Write down the exact amount you want to manifest. Know and believe that this amount is yours and yours alone.

Visualize yourself holding the money.

Did you write $10,000? Where would it come from? (The money may not come from that specific place; you only visualize to get the energy moving toward your goal.) What would you spend $10,000 on? Be clear and be precise.

Be the Person Who Creates the Money

If you want to attract money, you have to be the person who creates $10,000 monthly. Do what someone who creates $10,000 monthly would do.

Know the Law of Abundance

The Law of Abundance simply states that there is *plenty to go around*. There is more than enough wealth and money for everyone! It is just a matter of what you think and say so that you become a "wealth magnet." Here are some helpful positive affirmations for attracting money:

- *I am a money magnet.*
- *Money flows to me abundantly.*
- *I live in abundance and I enjoy sharing what I have.*

Learn to Visualize

Take time each day to see yourself enjoying the money. Feel it! Create vivid images and include pictures of your family cheering you on.

Visualization is an important step toward attracting the money you desire.

Create a Flowing Energy

Know that money is energy. That energy has to move! Learn to give back, knowing that it will return to you a hundred fold. When you give money to the needy, you are sending a message to your subconscious that you have enough, so you are able to give. By doing so, you attract the money you want.

Act!

Nothing happens until you act. You will not attract money if you don't work. Think of how you can become that person who creates money.

Stop Thinking Negatively

If you want to attract money, stay away from negative thoughts and limiting beliefs. Instead, think of and create positive affirmations.

Do you often find yourself thinking like this?

- *I can't afford that.*
- *I don't have enough money to purchase that.*
- *I have to work two jobs to get the money I want.*
- *That's too much; how can I afford that?*

Remember that the Law of Attraction says that you should focus your energy and attention on positive things. If you continue thinking negatively, you'll also attract negativity.

Continue to Move Forward

Keep moving toward achieving your goal. You might encounter challenges but you have to keep going. Take it one step at a time; it doesn't matter if you need to take one step forward and two steps back; continue moving forward.

Surround Yourself with Positive People

Do not associate yourself with people who will only suck the positive energy off you. You don't need these people. The main principle of the Law of Association is that *you become who you hang out with*. So to get great results, you have to associate with people who can lift you up in times when you need it most.

Follow Your Passion

Learn to love what you do. Follow your passion so that you attract the money you desire. Serve others and let money find you. People will be attracted to you if they can feel your passion for the things that you do.

CHAPTER 7

Powerful Affirmations to Attract Happiness

The power of the Law of Attraction works well when you use it with positive affirmations. Create happiness in your life by using the following powerful affirmations:

The Universe continues to support me.

Feeling alone, sometimes, is part of being human, but this affirmation tells you that you are never alone. The Universe is constantly orchestrating things for you, and you have to keep the faith. Focus on your goals and quit thinking that you are alone.

I am more than enough.

Do not think of yourself as inferior. You are more than enough. Your happiness does not depend on other people's approval. To be truly happy, you have to begin loving yourself again. Remember, you are always enough; don't let anyone tell you otherwise.

I have everything I need right now.

When your heart is full of thankfulness, there is inner happiness. Practice the act of being thankful for even the smallest things. Always look at what a situation, negative or positive, can do to your advantage. Practice gratitude, even if you are having a bad day. No matter what is going on around you, take a moment to reflect on all the things that you are grateful for; capture that feeling, and let that feeling see you through your day.

My heart radiates love.

Whatever you are going through, whether you are struggling with work or with your relationships, you will know that the best solution will always be based on love. Always remember that if you keep your heart open to receiving and radiating love, you will be happy.

My dreams are coming true.

Say this affirmation when you wake up and before you sleep to remind yourself that you are continuously fulfilling your dreams.

Happiness is not a destination; keep in mind that it is a way of life. Be happy now and watch your life change by using the power of the Law of Attraction.

Conclusion

Thank you again for purchasing this book! I really do hope you found it helpful.

If you enjoyed this book, then I'd like to ask you for a favor, would you be kind enough to leave a review for this book on Amazon?

It'd be greatly appreciated!